Contents

Structural Wonders

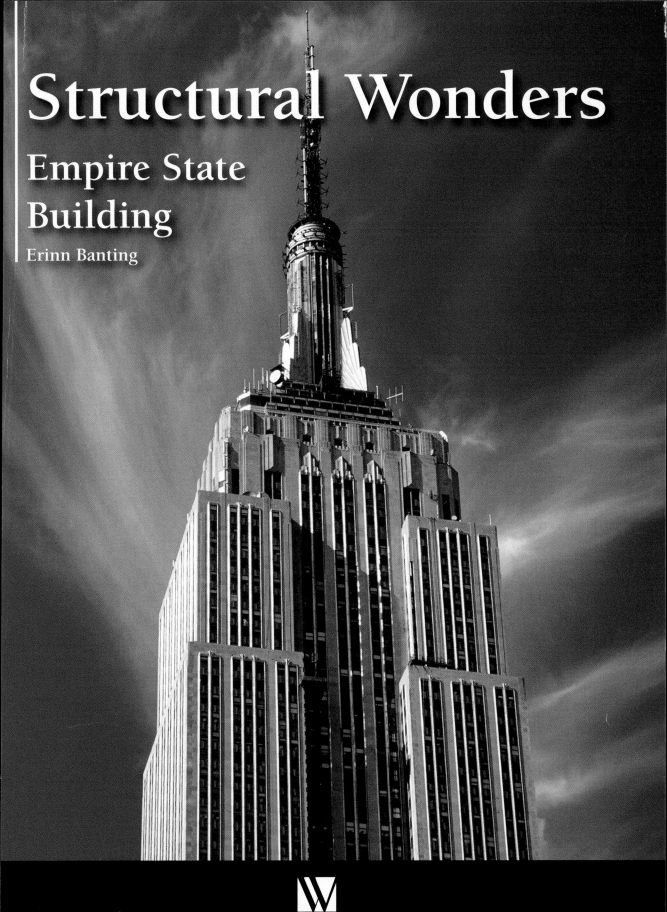

Structural Wonders

Empire State
Building

Erinn Banting

Published by Weigl Publishers Inc.
350 5th Avenue, Suite 3304, PMB 6G
New York, NY 10118-0069

Website: www.weigl.com

Library of Congress Cataloging-in-Publication Data

Banting, Erinn.
  Empire State Building / Erinn Banting.
     p. cm. -- (Structural wonders)
  Includes index.
  ISBN 978-1-59036-721-6 (hard cover : alk. paper) -- ISBN 978-1-59036-722-3 (soft cover :
alk. paper)
  1. Empire State Building (New York, N.Y.)--Design and construction--History--Juvenile literature. 2. New York (N.Y.)--Buildings, structures, etc.--Juvenile literature. I. Title.
  TH149.B35 2008
  720'.483097471--dc22
                         2007012112

Printed in the United States of America
1 2 3 4 5 6 7 8 9 0 11 10 09 08 07

Photograph Credits
Every reasonable effort has been made to trace ownership and to obtain
permission to reprint copyright material. The publishers would be pleased
to have any errors or omissions brought to their attention so that they may
be corrected in subsequent printings.

All of the internet URLs given in the book were valid at the time of publication.
However, due to the dynamic nature of the Internet, some addresses may have
changed, or sites may have ceased to exist since publication. While the author
and publisher regret any inconvenience this may cause readers, no responsibility
for any such changes can be accepted by either the author or the publisher.

Project Coordinators: Heather C. Hudak, Heather Kissock
Design: Terry Paulhus

What is the Empire State Building?

People have built structures for thousands of years. The tools, techniques, and materials they used have changed over time. However, the structures they built can be seen in cities and countries throughout the world. Houses, office buildings, towers, and monuments are all examples of structures.

Many structures are well known throughout the world. The Empire State Building in New York City is one of the world's most visited buildings. It was built in 1931, during a period known as the **Great Depression**. At this time, many people struggled to find jobs. The **investors** who funded the construction of the Empire State Building were able to carry on with their plans and gave work to thousands of people in need.

At 1,454 feet (443 meters), the Empire State Building set a world record as the world's tallest structure. Builders used an **assembly line** method for constructing the tower. This forever changed the way people raised buildings. Materials were pre-assembled off site to save time, builders worked in shifts around the clock, and construction took place on different levels of the building at the same time. The 102-story tower only took 1 year and 45 days to build.

Today, the New York City skyline would be hard to imagine without its skyscrapers. They serve as a reminder of the history, growth, and prosperity of one of the largest cities in the United States.

Quick Bites

- The Empire State Building appears in the King Kong movies.
- The Empire State Building has 73 elevators. Each moves 1,000 feet (305 m) per second. To travel from the lobby to the 86th floor takes less than one minute.
- At night, the top of the Empire State Building is lit up. Colored lights are used to represent different occasions. For example, on Valentine's Day, the lights are red. On Earth Day, they are green.

Building History

Through the early 1900s, New York was the center for industry, business, and culture. As a result, the state was given the nickname "The Empire State." People from around the world **immigrated** to New York in search of work and a better life. As the population grew, designers, planners, and **architects** had to find ways to make room for the growing number of people living and working in the busy city.

One way to solve the problem of limited space was to design buildings that stretched up into the sky, rather than spread out over wide areas. Before the 1800s, it was impossible to build structures over a certain height. The materials used were not strong enough to hold the building's weight. The development of steel and other sturdy materials meant that towers could reach to the sky.

In 1913, the Woolworth Building was the world's tallest building, at 57 stories.

Several large buildings were built in New York City. The term "skyscraper" was used to describe extremely tall towers. Companies competed to see who could build the tallest structure.

Construction of the Empire State Building took only 16 months.

TIMELINE OF CONSTRUCTION

1893: The original Waldorf Astoria Hotel is constructed on the present-day site of the Empire State Building.

1929: John Jakob Raskob and a group of investors form Empire State, Inc. and decide to build the world's tallest structure.

1930: Excavation of the site where the building now stands begins on January 22.

1930: Construction of the Empire State Building starts on March 17.

1931: The Empire State Building officially opens.

1972: The Empire State Building loses its title as "world's tallest building" with the construction of the World Trade Center towers, also in New York City.

1986: The Empire State Building is declared a National Historic Landmark by the U.S. government.

Crews worked around the clock to tear down the Waldorf Astoria Hotel, which was located on the site where the Empire State Building now stands.

In 1929, a businessman named John Jakob Raskob decided he wanted to construct the world's tallest structure. Work began in 1930. An architecture firm called Shreve, Lamb & Harmon Associates was hired to design the building. A company called Starrett Brothers and Eken was hired to build the tower. As time was tight, they decided to pre-build parts of the tower. Steel beams were made in Pennsylvania and shipped by boat, train, and truck. This saved time because the parts could be installed immediately upon arrival.

The total cost to construct the Empire State Building was $40,948,900, including land.

The Empire State Building was raised at record speed. Nearly one story was built each day. A crew of more than 3,400 workers worked seven days a week for nearly a year. In September 1930, the Empire State Building was declared the tallest building in the world. Although it was not finished, Raskob and his team had achieved their goal. Construction was completed in 1931, and the building remained the tallest in the world until 1972.

Structural Wonders

Lunchtime on a Skyscraper is a sculpture created as a tribute to the ironworkers who worked on structures such as the Empire State Building.

Big Ideas

In the 1900s, cities in the United States boomed. Architects and industry leaders wanted to build structures that represented the wealth and success of their companies. Towers grew taller, larger, and more elaborate. In cities such as Chicago and New York, architects competed to see whose tower could reach the highest.

When John Jakob Raskob set out to build the world's tallest building, he was in competition with many architects and designers. Raskob quickly set to work getting support for his project. He teamed up with the governor of New York State, Alfred E. Smith. As governor, Smith had a great deal of influence in New York City. Raskob also received help from a group of investors. Soon after, he hired Shreve, Lamb & Harmon Associates to develop the design concept for the building.

Building the tallest structure in the world took much planning and work. The building not only had to be the tallest, it also had to safe, attractive, and built in a very short period of time. William Lamb headed the project and worked on the design. Smith and Raskob gave Lamb freedom to design the building.

Lamb used a design style called Art Deco, which was popular at the time. Architects who worked in this style used **geometric** patterns, strong colors, and curving surfaces.

Web Link:
To find out more about Art Deco, go to www.decopix.com.

1) South Beach in Florida is known for its Art Deco District. 2) When the Chrysler Building was completed in 1930, it became the world's tallest structure. 3) The Washington Monument was the world's tallest structure between 1884 and 1888.

Profile:
Shreve, Lamb & Harmon Associates

The firm hired to design the Empire State Building, Shreve, Lamb & Harmon Associates, was well known for building office towers in New York. The partnership was founded in 1929 by Canadian architect Richmond Harold Shreve and American architects William Lamb and Arthur Loomis Harmon.

Shreve was born in the Canadian province of Nova Scotia in 1877 and studied architecture at Cornell University in New York. After graduating in 1902, he taught at the university for four years before joining the firm of Carrère and Hastings. The firm was one of the most successful in New York City and was known for its design of important buildings, such as the New York Public Library.

William Lamb was born in Brooklyn, New York, in 1883. He studied architecture at New York's Columbia University, and later, at Ecole des Beaux-Arts in Paris. In 1911, he joined Carrère and Hastings. In 1920, Lamb and Shreve became partners in Carrère and Hastings. Together, they worked on many of the firm's projects, including the Standard Oil Building, an early skyscraper completed in 1922. In 1924, Shreve and Lamb left Carrère and Hastings to create their own firm.

THE WORK OF SHREVE, LAMB & HARMON ASSOCIATES

500 Fifth Avenue

500 Fifth Avenue was built in 1930 at the corner of Fifth Avenue and 42nd Street in New York City. The design of the building was inspired by the Empire State Building. As it rises to its 60 stories, the tower tapers.

The Mutual of New York Building

The Mutual of New York Building was built in 1950 for the Mutual of New York Insurance Company. It is known for its unique top—a tower that rises above the 25-story building. At the top of the tower there is a digital screen that shows the air temperature and a sign that reads "MONY," which are the initials of the building's owner.

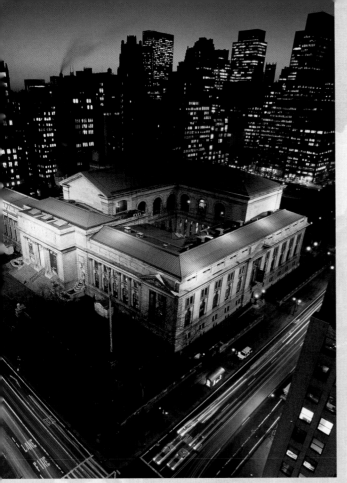

More than 15 million people visit the New York Public Library each year.

Arthur Loomis Harmon was born in Chicago in 1878. Harmon studied at the Art Institute of Chicago and Columbia University. He graduated in 1901 and went on to work at many New York-based architecture firms. In 1929, he joined Shreve & Lamb. This was around the time the firm was hired to design the Empire State Building.

As head designer, Lamb had to rely on an expert and skilled contracting company. The team hired Starrett Brothers and Eken, an experienced contracting firm in New York City. They had worked on many other buildings, including the Metropolitan Life North Building and 40 Wall Street, which is now known as The Trump Building.

Starrett Brothers and Eken told the investors that, to raise a tower of the Empire State Building's size in a short amount of time, they would have to buy or design new equipment. They convinced the investors it would be more efficient to buy new cranes, machines, and supplies that they could sell once construction was complete.

3 Park Avenue

3 Park Avenue was built in 1976 in New York City. The building is unique because, instead of facing the street, it is turned on an angle. It also has buttresses. Buttresses are built to give buildings extra support.

Glass Center Building at the 1939 World's Fair in New York City

The Glass Center was built to display glass from three companies. The building was 108 feet (33m) high and had 25,000 square feet (2,323 square meters) of floor space. It was made from blue plate glass and glass blocks.

The Science Behind the Building

The designers and builders who created the Empire State building had to have a good understanding of science to build the world's largest structure. They had to know the correct materials to use and how to put the building together in a way that guaranteed stability and strength.

Loads

A **load** is a force that impacts how a structure must be built. Designers and architects must take loads into consideration when building a tower, such as the Empire State Building. Buildings are constructed to withstand loads. There are different kinds of loads that architects and designers have to consider before construction begins.

The weight of the building, including all the materials needed to build it, is called the dead load. Architects must consider additional weight from items such as furniture and people. These add weight to the structure and are included in what is called the live load. The kind of soil where the building is constructed is also important. Soil can sometimes shift or move after construction is complete. The degree to which a building shifts is called the settlement load.

Steel columns and beams form a three-dimensional grid in the structure of the building.

Climate plays a role in the design and construction process. The thermal load refers to the degree to which a building will shrink or expand in different temperatures. Hot temperatures cause materials to expand. Cold temperatures cause them to contract. In some places, earthquakes are common. Earthquake loads pull horizontally on structures. Wind loads are also important to consider. The force of the wind blowing against a structure impacts how it is constructed.

Tension and Compression

To make a building that will survive the forces of nature, architects must consider the forces of **tension** and **compression**. Tension pulls materials apart. It acts in the opposite way to compression, which pushes materials together. Wind loads create both compression and tension. The side of the building that is being blown against is acted upon by tension, while the opposite side is acted upon by compression. The grid-like design of the Empire State Building helped to resist the tension and compression created by the wind load. The designers used steel to construct the building because it is known to resist compression. Each steel beam was fastened on all sides, including the top and bottom. This meant that each cube in the frame had a limited range of movement. Even in winds up to 110 miles per hour, the building only moves 1.48 inches (3.76 centimeters). When it was constructed, the designers of the Empire State Building said it would take 4.5 million pounds of pressure from a heavy wind to knock over the tower.

Web Link:
To find out more about how skyscrapers are built, visit www.allaboutskyscrapers.com/ skyscraper_construction.htm.

Science and Technology

Constructing the tallest structure in the world took planning, labor, and the latest technology. The designers, architects, and laborers that worked on the Empire State Building used special tools, materials, and methods. Many of these tools and methods operate under basic principles of science.

Pulleys

Large cranes were used to lift heavy steel beams up to each floor and to put the beams in place. Cranes use pulleys to move heavy objects. Pulleys change the direction of the force, making it easier to lift things. Pulleys use wheels wrapped in rope or wire. On one end of the rope is a hook that attaches to the object that needs to be lifted. On the other end, a person pulls the rope. The pulley uses a wheel to help distribute the weight, making it feel lighter so it can be moved.

Workers lift objects using pulleys.

Girders, or large steel beams, are often put in place using cranes.

Steam Engines

Enormous shovels were used to dig the giant pit where the **foundation** was built. These machines were powered by steam engines. Invented in the 1700s, steam engines were used in factories, vehicles, and machinery. The operation of the engines relied on a system that used water and **pistons**. Water was heated in large boilers, which created steam. The steam expanded and compressed in the engine. The compressed steam moved a piece called a piston. The movement of the piston was connected to the moving parts of the engine, which forced the engines to go. Using steam-powered shovels saved a great deal of time and helped move along the construction of the Empire State Building.

Crowbars are useful when opening large crates.

Levers

Before construction on the Empire State Building began, the Waldorf-Astoria Hotel had to be torn down. With a tight schedule for construction, workers had to **demolish** the hotel while they excavated the site of the new tower. Workers called "barmen" used tools called crowbars to tear down the building. Crowbars use a principle of science called a lever. A lever is a simple machine used to move a load around a pivot using a force. Workers used crowbars to grip nails. Using the crowbar's rounded head as the pivot, workers applied force to the long arm. This pried nails loose that would otherwise have been impossible to remove by hand.

Quick Bites

- It is estimated that 365,000 tons (331,000 tonnes) of dirt and rock were dug from the Empire State Building's construction site.
- Each week, 4.5 stories of the Empire State Building were constructed.
- The Empire State Building has 102 flights of stairs, with 1,860 steps.

Computer-Aided Design

Architects are trained professionals who work with clients to design structures. Before anything is built, they make detailed drawings or models. These plans are important tools that help people visualize what the structure will look like. A blueprint is a detailed diagram that shows where all the parts of the structure will be placed. Walls, doors, windows, plumbing, electrical wiring, and other details are mapped out on the blueprint. Blueprints act as a guide for engineers and builders during construction.

For centuries, architects and builders worked without the aid of computers. Sketches and blueprints were drawn by hand. Highly skilled drafters would draw very technical designs. Today, this process is done using computers and sophisticated software programs. Architects use CAD, or computer-aided design, throughout the design process. Early CAD systems used computers to draft building plans. Today's computer programs can do much more. They can build three-dimensional models and computer simulations of how a building will look. They can also calculate the effects of different physical forces on the structure. Using CAD, today's architects can build more complex structures at lower cost and in less time.

Computer-aided design programs have been used since the 1960s.

Eye on Design

Computer-Aided Design and the Guggenheim Museum, New York

Frank Lloyd Wright designed the Guggenheim Museum in New York. The white building resembles the shell of a snail.

Technology has been used to create buildings based on the designs of architects from the past. Frank Lloyd Wright is an American architect. His designs have been built in the United States and Europe. The homes he designed were built with materials from their surroundings so that they complemented the environment. During his lifetime, he designed more than 1,100 buildings. Only half were ever built. Since his death, different architects have revived his designs and built structures based on them.

In 2004, architect Thomas A. Heinz began working on a house that Wright had designed in the early 1950s. Heinz had four sketches of the design. He used a software program called ArchiCAD to build a model of the house. ArchiCAD helps architects build models piece by piece. It also allows them to run reports that detail design features such as windows, doors, electrical outlets, and other fixtures. Heinz based his model on Wright's sketches and on his knowledge of Wright's design style. Without the help of a computer, the house might never have been constructed.

MEASURING THE EMPIRE STATE BUILDING

Location

The building is in New York City, New York. There are five entrances. They are located on 33rd Street, Fifth Avenue, and 34th Street.

Height

- 1,454 feet (443 m) to top of lightning rod
- 1,050 feet (320 m) to the 86th floor observatory
- 1,224 feet (373 m) to the 102nd floor tower
- 230 feet (70 m) from the 102nd floor to the tip
- 204 feet (62 m) is the antenna height

Area

East to west, the building is 424 feet (129 m). North to south, the building is 187 feet (57 m).

Weight

The building weighs 365,000 tons (331,000 tonnes).

Other Interesting Facts

- 6,500 windows
- Took a total of 7 million work hours to construct

Movement

The building moves 1.48 inches (3.76 cm) in high wind.

Environmental Viewpoint

Constructing a tower as large as the Empire State Building had a significant effect on New York City. It changed the face of the New York skyline and impacted the city and the people who lived there.

During the race to build the world's largest structure in the 1900s, some people were concerned about how the towers might impact the natural environment. Before the Chrysler Building and the Empire State Building were constructed, the Eiffel Tower in Paris, France, was the world's tallest tower. Some people did not want the tower to be built. They thought it might damage surrounding parkland and ruin the skyline of the city. In some European cities, such as London, the construction of skyscrapers was restricted because people thought the new structures would overshadow the view of historical buildings.

In New York, the tallest tower was viewed as a symbol of power and strength. The Empire State Building was one of many enormous towers to crop up in New York over the next 100 years. Although there was a drive to grow the city, the government of New York had created laws to restrict the types of towers that could be built. William Lamb had to design a building that tapered, or became thinner as it grew in height. This was so that the massive tower did not block all the smaller buildings surrounding it.

Even though the Empire State Building is now surrounded by higher and more modern buildings, it still known throughout the world as one of New York's most important historic landmarks.

Today, the Empire State Building is one of New York's most recognized features. The city and the people who work in the building work hard to preserve their important landmark. In 1986, the tower was declared a landmark by the New York Preservation Commission, which works to protect historical buildings. More than 250 people monitor the tower on a daily basis. This helps prevent things such as tourism and weather from causing permanent damage.

Restoration projects have been completed to ensure the building is preserved, safe, and efficient. In the late 1980s, crews evaluated the damage to the facade, or face, of the building caused by **acid rain**, wind, and humidity. Many parts of the facade were replaced or repaired to prevent further damage.

ENERGY EFFICIENCY

The owners and managers of the Empire State Building work to ensure the building does not have a negative effect on its surrounding environment. At one time, heat and air were escaping from the building. This decreased the building's energy efficiency.

In the 1990s, the 6,500 windows of the tower were replaced. This made the building more energy efficient by reducing the amount of air coming into and out of the building.

Other changes to make the building more energy efficient included replacing more than 30,000 light bulbs with ones that conserve energy, changing the heating and air conditioning systems, and updating the water pumps.

Construction Careers

The investors, architects, and designers who had the vision to build the Empire State Building were important to its creation. Without the workers who helped build it, however, the building would have remained a blueprint.

In order to win the race to construct the world's tallest structure, thousands of workers were needed. At the peak of construction, about 3,400 people worked on the building at the same time. In total, it took 7 million working hours to complete the massive project. More than 60,000 tons (54,000 tonnes) of steel, 62,000 cubic yards (47,400 cubic meters) of concrete, and 200,000 cubic feet (1,756 cubic meters) of limestone and granite were used to build the tower. Crews worked around-the-clock to construct the building.

Riveting teams

Riveting teams put **rivets** in place. These teams were important to the construction of the Empire State Building. Each riveting team included a "heater," a "catcher," a "bucker-up," and a "gunman." The heater put the rivets in an oven called a forge until they were red hot. Using tongs that

were 3 feet (1 m) long, the heater would throw the rivets up to the catcher, who waited on the floors above. Catchers used old tins to catch the fiery rivets. Once they caught a rivet, they would quickly pick it up with another set of tongs and put it through the holes of the beams that needed to be fastened. The bucker-up held the rivet steady so the gunman could hammer it into place with a special riveting hammer. As the rivet cooled down, it fused, or melted together, with the beam to form a strong and permanent seal.

Lifting crews

Lifting crews used cranes to move the heavy steel beams. The men that made up these crews were called derrick operators. A derrick is a type of large crane that is used to lift, move, and place heavy objects. A derrick operator uses levers and pedals to move the boom, which is the long rod at the top of the crane. Often, derrick operators help maintain and clean the equipment, and help set up at new sites. During construction of the Empire State Building, derricks were used to hoist and place enormous steel beams.

Steelworkers

Steel is much stronger than iron, and it is used in many structures, including the Empire State Building. Steelworkers manufacture steel.

Steel is made by refining iron. Refined iron is heated so that other impurities, such as carbon, are removed. The refined iron is called steel. Large amounts of oxygen are blasted through powerful furnaces. The oxygen combines with the carbon in the iron.

Web Link:
To find out more about steelworkers, visit www.uswa.com/uswa/program/content/index.php.

Notable Structures

The race to build the world's tallest structure did not end when the Empire State Building took the title in 1931. Many other architects continued to look for new ways, materials, and designs that would surpass the Empire State Building's 102 stories.

Sears Tower

Construction completed: 1973

Location: Chicago, United States

Architect: Bruce Graham

Description: Plans for the Sears Tower began in 1969. At the time, Sears Roebuck & Co. operated one of the largest chains of department stores in the United States. The company built the tower for its 350,000 employees. The 1,450-foot (442-m) tall building has more office space than any tower in the United States.

Petronas Towers

Construction completed: 1998

Location: Kuala Lumpur, Malaysia

Architect: César Pelli

Description: Both of the Petronas Towers rise to a height of 1,483 feet (452 m). The design of the towers was inspired by the art of a religion called Islam. Although they look identical, the two towers were built by two different construction companies. The companies competed to see who could raise their tower the fastest.

The Empire State Building remained the tallest structure for more than 40 years. It is now considered one of the great landmarks of New York City.

Jin Mao Tower

Construction completed: 1998

Location: Shanghai, China

Architect: Skidmore, Owings & Merrill

Description: The design of the Jin Mao Tower was inspired by Chinese architecture. The octagon-shaped building tapers as it stretches into the sky. Due to its location, the tower was built with special reinforcements to protect it from collapse in extreme weather or during earthquakes.

Taipei 101

Construction completed: 2004

Location: Taipei, Taiwan

Architect: C.Y. Lee and Partners

Description: At 1,670 feet (509 m), Taipei 101 is currently the tallest building in the world. The building, which resembles a stick of bamboo, was built based on the number eight. Each of the eight sections of the building has eight floors. The number eight is considered lucky by many Chinese people.

Tall Buildings Through History

For centuries, people have strived to build the world's tallest structures. Prior to 1889, when the Eiffel Tower was built, there were no structures reaching more than 1,000 feet (305 m).

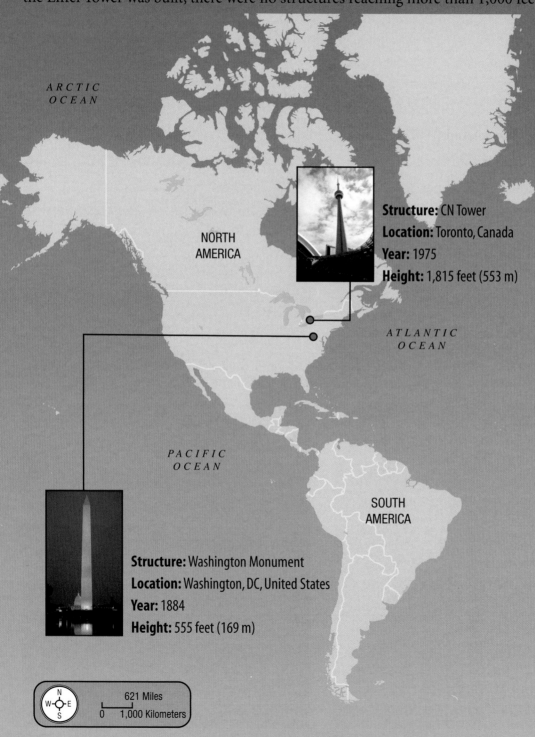

ARCTIC
OCEAN

NORTH
AMERICA

Structure: CN Tower
Location: Toronto, Canada
Year: 1975
Height: 1,815 feet (553 m)

ATLANTIC
OCEAN

PACIFIC
OCEAN

SOUTH
AMERICA

Structure: Washington Monument
Location: Washington, DC, United States
Year: 1884
Height: 555 feet (169 m)

621 Miles
0   1,000 Kilometers

However, with better technology, these structures could rise higher. This map shows some of the world's highest structures throughout history.

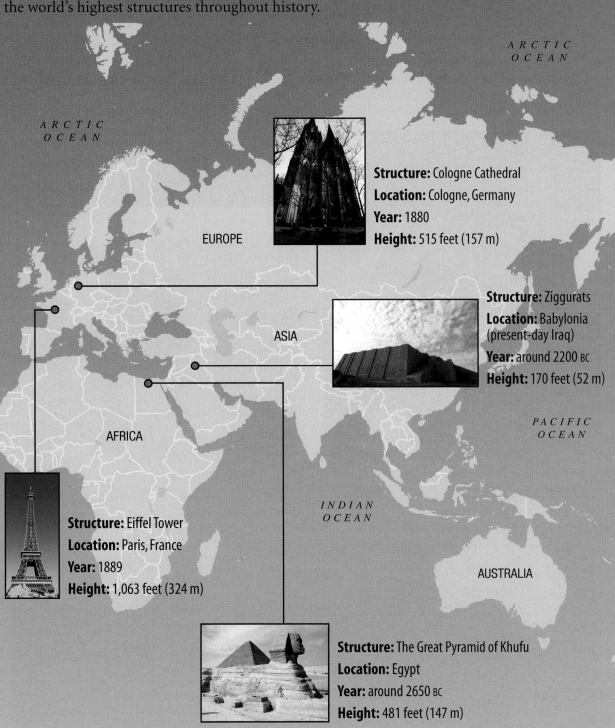

Structure: Cologne Cathedral
Location: Cologne, Germany
Year: 1880
Height: 515 feet (157 m)

Structure: Ziggurats
Location: Babylonia (present-day Iraq)
Year: around 2200 BC
Height: 170 feet (52 m)

Structure: Eiffel Tower
Location: Paris, France
Year: 1889
Height: 1,063 feet (324 m)

Structure: The Great Pyramid of Khufu
Location: Egypt
Year: around 2650 BC
Height: 481 feet (147 m)

Quiz

Q What is computer-aided design (CAD)?

A Computer-aided design is a system that lets architects draft structural designs by computer. Sophisticated software programs allow designers to view the structure in three dimensions and simulate how the structure will work.

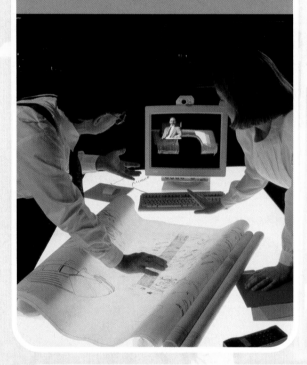

Q What was the Empire State Building named after?

A It was named after New York State's nickname— the Empire State.

Q What was the role of a gunman on a riveting team?

A The gunman hammered the rivet into place with a special riveting hammer.

Q What is a load?

A A load is a force that impacts how a structure must be built.

Activity

Architects and designers use blueprints to plan their buildings. Blueprints include overall images of the size and shape of the building, as well as the interior of the building. Floor plans show each of the rooms on each of a building's floors. Using a few simple tools, design a floor plan.

Materials
- Graph paper
- A ruler
- A pencil
- An eraser
- A blue or black marker

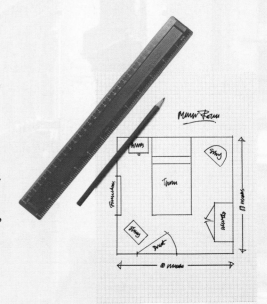

Instructions

First, decide what kind of building you would like to design. It could be a house, an apartment block, a school, an office building, or a shopping center. Then, make a list of all the rooms that will be inside the building.

1. Start by designing the main room on the first floor. Decide where it should be located, how big it should be, and how it will connect to other rooms. Each square on the graph paper is equal to one square foot (0.1 sq m) in a room.

2. Using a ruler and a pencil, trace the outline of the room. Add doors and windows using the special symbols that architects use. These symbols can be viewed at **www.stanfordartedventures.com/create/ try_this_floorplan.htm**.

3. Draw the remaining rooms. Make sure they connect to one another. Look at how many entrances and exits are needed. Does the building need bathrooms or a kitchen? Think about whether your building needs stairs or an elevator up to the next floor. Add these things to your floor plan.

4. Once the floor plan is complete, trace over the pencil lines with marker. Now, the blueprint is complete.

Further Research

You can find more information on the Empire State Building, skyscrapers, and the world's tallest structures at your local library or on the Internet.

Websites

For more information on the Empire State Building, visit
http://www.esbnyc.com/kids

For more information on skyscrapers, visit
http://science.howstuffworks.com/skyscraper5.htm

For more information on the world's tallest structures, visit
http://www.emporis.com/en/bu/sk/st/tp/wo/

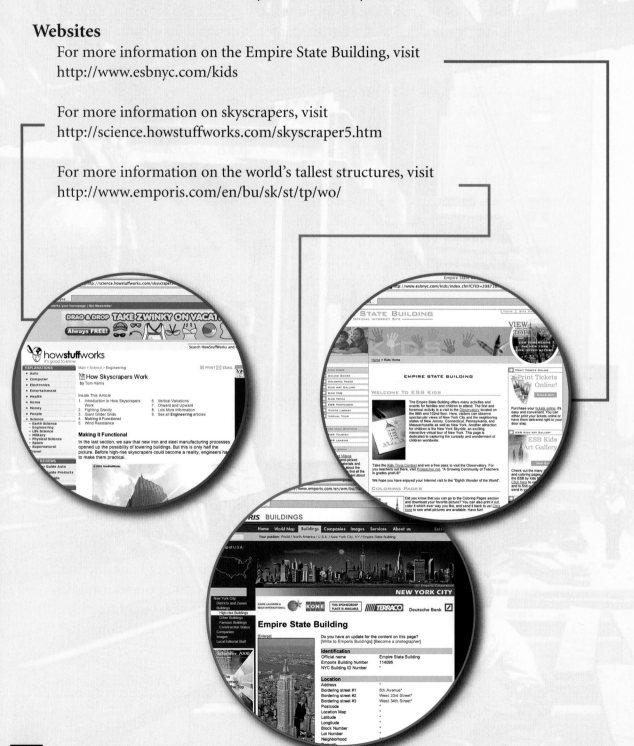

Glossary

acid rain: precipitation containing pollution that can harm the environment

architects: people who design and supervise the construction of buildings

assembly line: a sequence of machines, tools, workers, and operations in a factory, arranged so that at each stage a further process is carried out

compression: the act of being flattened or squeezed together by pressure

demolish: the act of tearing down a building

foundation: the part of a building that helps support its weight

geometric: pertaining to a type of mathematics that deals with the relationships between points, lines, and angles

Great Depression: a period during the 1930s when many people lost their jobs

immigrated: moved or settled in another country or region

investors: people who support a project with money

load: a weight or source of pressure carried by an object

pistons: discs that slide back and forth in a hollow cylinder

rivets: metal items which are used to fasten large pieces of metal together

tension: the state of being stretched

Index